Ready, SET, GO!
Sports of All Sorts

¡En sus marcas, LISTOS, FUERA!
Deportes de todo tipo

Written by · Escrito por
Celeste Cortright

Illustrated by · Ilustrado por
Christiane Engel

Translated by · Traducido por
Aidelyz Ruiz Robles

Barefoot Books
step inside a story

We're **ready** for action and all **set** for fun.
Let's **GO** and get ready to play, everyone!

¡Que empiece la acción! ¡Listos para la diversión!
¡Prepárense ya, que el juego comenzó!

Warming up at the **track**, we stretch down to the ground,
Then get our hearts pumping by jogging around.
We line up in lanes, and then, ready, set... RUN!
We zoom to the finish! The race has begun.

En la **pista**, nos estiramos hasta el suelo y calentamos los músculos.
Nos paramos de nuevo, y trotamos sin obstáculos.
Nos organizamos en los carriles, en sus marcas, listos ...¡CORRAN!
¡Fijados en la meta! ¡La carrera empieza ahora!

Let's do **gymnastics** and fly through the air.
We tumble and cartwheel with power and flair.
We try to stay balanced and stick all our landings,
And cheer on our teammates for being outstanding!

Hagamos **gimnasia**, volando por el aire.
Dando vueltas y piruetas como si fuese baile.
Con buen equilibrio caemos de pie.
¡Felices porque lo logramos muy bien!

Wearing our jerseys and **baseball** caps,
Each one of us takes a swing with the bat.
We send the ball flying and set a quick pace,
Working hard as we can to reach the next base.

Luciendo nuestras camisetas y gorras de **béisbol**,
Cada vez bateando la pelota mejor.
Bateamos la pelota y la hacemos volar.
Corriendo hasta la próxima base alcanzar.

We dive in the water and make a big splash!
Kicking fast with our legs, **swimming** by in a flash.
We work on our strokes in the glistening pool,
Then we rest and we float and the water feels cool.

¡Nos zambullimos en el agua dando un gran chapuzón!
Aleteando y pateando, **nadamos** veloz.
Practicamos nuestras brazadas en el agua cristalina.
Flotamos y descansamos, se siente fresca la piscina.

Some call it **football** and some call it **soccer**.
The forwards love scoring; the goalie's the blocker.
We zip down the field as we kick at the ball,
Using feet, knees and bodies — but no hands at all!

Algunos le llaman **fútbol** y otros le llaman **balompié**,
Los delanteros anotan puntos, si el portero no bloquea bien.
Corremos por el campo, y pateamos el balón.
Usamos pies, rodillas o cuerpos, pero las manos no.

It's time to play **hockey** — excitement awaits!
We put on our helmets and lace up our skates.
Skating the ice rink takes care and control.
We pass the puck down towards the other team's goal.

Jugamos al **hockey**: ¡que la emoción no termine!

Nos ponemos nuestros cascos y nos atamos los patines.

Con balance y control se patina en el hielo.

Le pegamos al disco y anotamos en el juego.

When we're at **karate**, our work is intense.

We learn self-control and we gain confidence.

From white belt to black belt, our skill slowly grows.

With focus and patience, we'll all feel like pros!

Practicando **kárate**, es intenso el esfuerzo.
Aprender control propio, es tan solo el comienzo.
De cinta blanca a cinta negra, nuestra habilidad crece lentamente.
Nos sentiremos expertos, si nos enfocamos pacientemente.

On the **basketball** court, the pace is quite fast.

When we hear *"I'm open!"*, we turn and we pass.

We dribble the ball and we work up a sweat.

We shoot and then — *swish!* It goes straight in the net!

En la cancha de **baloncesto**, rápido todos vamos.

Al escuchar "¡Estoy abierto!", nos giramos y el balón pasamos.

Driblamos el balón, y terminamos sudando.

Tiramos el balón ¡Fuah! Estamos encestando.

All over the world, kids love to play.
What kind of **sport** will you try out today?

En cualquier parte del mundo, los niños quieren jugar.
¿Qué tipo de **deporte** intentaras practicar?

Track and Field · Atletismo

A running race was the only event at the first ancient Olympic Games in Greece! Today people in over 200 countries enjoy events like sprinting, hurdling and relay races, making track and field the second most popular sport in the world.

¡Una carrera a pie fue el único evento en los primeros Juegos Olímpicos de la antigua Grecia! Hoy en día, en más de 200 países, la gente disfruta de eventos como carreras de velocidad, carreras de obstáculos y carreras de relevos, lo cual convierte al atletismo en el segundo deporte más popular del mundo.

Gymnastics · Gimnasia

Gymnasts perform acts of balance, strength and flexibility. They perform for a panel of judges who give them a score based on how well they do their routines. Gymnastics is popular in Russia, Romania, China, the United States and beyond.

Los gimnastas realizan actos de equilibrio, fuerza y flexibilidad. Compiten frente a un panel de jueces que les otorgan una puntuación basada en qué tan bien hacen sus rutinas. La gimnasia es popular en Rusia, Rumania, China, los Estados Unidos y más allá.

Baseball · Béisbol

In this team sport, players take turns striking a ball with a bat and then running around the field to all four bases to score. Baseball is the national sport of both Cuba and the United States, and also the most popular sport in Japan and Venezuela.

En este deporte de equipo, para anotar, los jugadores toman turnos golpeando una pelota con un bate, y luego corren alrededor del campo hacia las cuatro bases. El béisbol es el deporte nacional de Cuba y de los Estados Unidos. También es el deporte más popular en Japón y en Venezuela.

Swimming · Natación

Competitive swimming began in England, the home of the first public swimming pool. People all around the world swim for fun and for sport. In Australia, almost half of all the people who live there consider themselves to be swimmers!

La natación competitiva comenzó en Inglaterra, el hogar de la primera piscina pública. Personas alrededor del mundo nadan para divertirse y para practicar el deporte. En Australia, ¡casi la mitad de toda la gente que vive allí se consideran nadadores!

Football/Soccer · Fútbol/Balompié

This sport is the most popular game in the world, played by people from more than 200 countries. Two teams of eleven players compete to get the ball past the goalkeeper into the other team's net without using their hands or arms.

Este deporte es el juego más popular del mundo y es jugado por personas de más de 200 países. Dos equipos de once jugadores compiten para lograr que el balón pase al portero y alcance la red del otro equipo sin usar sus manos o sus brazos.

Ice Hockey · Hockey sobre hielo

In ice hockey, two teams of ice skaters score points by using sticks to shoot a rubber disk called a puck into the other team's net. Ice hockey is Canada's national sport, and the game is also popular in the United States as well as northern Europe.

En el hockey sobre hielo, dos equipos de patinadores de hielo anotan puntos, usando palos para tirar un disco de goma hacia la red del otro equipo. El hockey sobre hielo es el deporte nacional de Canadá. Este juego también es popular en los Estados Unidos y en el norte de Europa.

Karate · Kárate

Karate began in Japan but is now enjoyed by people all around the world. Karate involves learning a series of moves that are graded by teachers to earn different belts — starting from white and working up to black.

El kárate comenzó en Japón, pero ahora lo disfrutan personas de todo el mundo. El kárate implica aprender una serie de movimientos que son calificados por los maestros para ganar diferentes cintas. Comienzan con la cinta blanca hasta llegar a la negra.

Basketball · Baloncesto

When basketball was first invented, it was played with a soccer ball and a peach basket! Now two teams of five players bounce an orange ball around the court, shooting it into a net basket to score points.

Cuando se inventó el baloncesto, ¡se jugaba con una balón de fútbol y una canasta de duraznos! Hoy en día, para anotar, dos equipos de cinco jugadores rebotan un balón naranja a través de la cancha y la lanzan a un cesto de red.

To Mom & Dad,
for always cheering me on — C. C.

Para mi mamá y mi papá,
por siempre regalarme ánimos — C.C.

For you, the reader of this book! Stay awesome — C. E.

¡Para ti, lector o lectora de este libro!
No pares de ser genial — C. E.

Barefoot Books
23 Bradford Street, 2nd Floor
Concord, MA 01742

Barefoot Books
29/30 Fitzroy Square
London, W1T 6LQ

Text copyright © 2020 by Celeste Cortright
Illustrations copyright © 2020 by Christiane Engel
The moral rights of Celeste Cortright and
Christiane Engel have been asserted

First published in United States of America by Barefoot Books, Inc
and in Great Britain by Barefoot Books, Ltd in 2020
This bilingual Spanish paperback edition
first published in 2021. All rights reserved

Graphic design by Sarah Soldano, Barefoot Books
Edited and art directed by Kate DePalma, Barefoot Books
Translated by Aidelyz Ruiz Robles
Reproduction by Bright Arts, Hong Kong
Printed in China on 100% acid-free paper
This book was typeset in Adriatic, Charter and Sassoon Infant
The illustrations were prepared in acrylic,
water-based paints and digital collage

ISBN 978-1-64686-428-7

British Cataloguing-in-Publication Data:
a catalogue record for this book is available
from the British Library

Library of Congress Cataloging-in-Publication Data for
the English edition is available under LCCN 2019043262

1 3 5 7 9 8 6 4 2

The publisher would like to thank the many expert reviewers
who helped ensure the accuracy of this book, including school
wellness researcher Scott Greenspan and inclusivity specialist Anne Cohen.

El editor quisiera agradecerle a los revisores expertos por ayudar a
asegurar la precisión de este libro, incluyendo al investigador de bienestar
escolar Scott Greenspan y a la especialista de inclusividad Anne Cohen.